Yellow Shade

Yellow Shade

Dimakatso Sedite

ISBN 978-1-928476-38-2
ebook ISBN 978-1-928476-39-9

Deep South, Makhanda
contact@deepsouth.co.za
www.deepsouth.co.za

Distributed in South Africa by
Blue Weaver Marketing and Distribution
https://blueweaver.co.za

Distributed worldwide by
African Books Collective
PO Box 721, Oxford, OX1 9EN, UK
www.africanbookscollective.com/publishers/deep-south

Earlier versions of some of these poems were published in the following
journals, anthologies and writer blogs: *Aerodrome*, *Botsotso*, *New Coin*,
Brittle Paper, *Teesta Review*, *Kalahari Review*, *Poéfrika* and *Hello Poetry*.

Cover art: Sam Nhlengethwa, "My Grandmother's Kitchen in the 60s"
hand-printed lithograph, Published by The Artists' Press
Cover design: Gugulethu Nangamso Mtumane
Text design and layout: Liz Gowans

Contents

I

II

III

IV

I

Middle-town

Born from my mother's warmth, I seemed to amble in this egg
that scrubbed pots and rode a bicycle to work.
I'd suck my fingers till they tasted like cloth.
Growing up in middle-town, clouds looked for an excuse to split
and flee my plainness; my cropped carpet hair echoed my muteness,
which crawled into a classroom filled with whipping canes,
and many songs we sang to make us forget we had no textbooks.
After school, we'd stop by Ntate Moruti, to speak more songs,
about Bethlehem, Judea, our cartilage selves breaking locust legs
of his bench, as we waited for peaches on his tree to redden.

Being homesick means looking through your keyhole of childhood,
to find shiny water buckets missing you.
You become a box breaking into pieces to squat
on a sugar bowl, on a time-washed table, on melamine floors.
Faith hangs like a spider web on Jesus' Cross,
next to the arms of a dead clock that guards these mute things
that refuse to die with us. Limbs of an apple tree
whip the roof's gutters with stories, as the sun's wreckage
lands on the buttocks of dishes in the sink.

Feeling empty is returning to a textbook of friends long snatched
by an illness so ruthless, you could hear their young veins break,
leaving the wind alone to deal with a lorry of grief.
Growing old is a basket cracking your mind everywhere,
sniffing at an hour when friends stopped calling,
as they intrude into your memories like trees.
Ageing is watching your children needing you less and less,
as your bad poems sink into themselves,
as your cloth of defeat trails behind.

Being helpless is watching my mother forget how to
button a shirt – how to hold important things together –
as time stands between her and the mist.
It's hearing a night with my man tear up into a glass of day,
or watching his heart crash into a younger woman's chest,
and knowing there is nothing I can do about it.

Far from home

The monsoon Gautrain carries phantoms to work,
shatters a night-clock hanging from the sky's roof.
Commuters are hard-boiled yolks inside this soundless bullet.
Eyes melt Tselane's phone screen, it changes with landscapes,
her face mole-less, skirting the edge of a seat.

Later they froth out of the station's ears, in a stillness only seen
in underwater zones. Buildings reeking of deadlines suck them up,
morph them into desk muffins. They prod the wagon westward,
dragging the hours mounting its horns, to get done, get paid,
and start the cycle again, the next day.

Images on her phone are faster than the train.
She video-calls her father, realises how cold her hands are,
like those of a woman who's found love late. Dirty dishes
do the fighting for her: forks sticking out, bowls squatting,
as she sinks the weight of her office clock into her sofa.

In Matatiele, the dying sun warms the knob of her father's thôbane,
his palm gripping its scratchy wood, to steady his frailness.
A fedora hides the grey bush growing on his brows.
As they video-chat, dusk clings to his window frame, healing its crack.

My mother's skirt

Your floral skirt lies on my chair,
graceful, echoing colours
of my room – green, blue, yellow –
colours that remind me of your warmth,
a comforting blanket.
I hear you shuffling down the passage,
knees bent. I smell vetkoek and salted snoek.
Blackie's wet nose peeps in.

Your skirt, an umbrella bursting with colour,
covers your arthritic knees and burnt ankles.
How is it possible to love someone
whose fate is to leave her favourite skirt
and me behind?
My tears dot your skirt like rooibos tea.
The silence of your presence is a radio
of memories that will not switch off.
I touch the cold garden on your skirt.
All I see is the shape of your hand in mine.

The lure of liquid delight

My babies huddle in warmth,
candle licking their breath.
I tiptoe to the outside,
to dip my lips in skomfana,
to twist a hip to floating songs.

Mamoriti staggers like a wheelbarrow,
'Your shack's on fire!'
Golden tongues beat the darkness.
I knock down my tin of liquid delight,
gust like an ostrich towards my house.

Men with buckets fight fists of flames,
fear burns my nose, clings to my dress,
smoke wraps around my face. My eyes
are torches looking for my children.

I'm twisting in disbelief when Mamoriti's
fleshy hand pulls my knotted guts towards
a mangled fence, where my babies stand,
alive.

The convent

We were growing our bones, raised by bunk-beds,
our dorm windows bare, wrapped in an album of mountains.
On Tuesdays we were allowed to remember we were children,
flashed the sun's eyes with our cheeks, sniffed our fleeting childhood.
Our cotton balls of black hair flipped with our wooden legs
in the freedom of the open air no-one dared to claim,
before burning our brittle skulls between thighs of books again,
staring at a future so distant it knew the stars' great-aunts
by their middle names.

We were doll-dressed, parcel-packed into suitcases,
to be raised by nuns, hymns, mountains
and memories of our mothers' love.
We tumbled out later, pencil-firm, to a whale
of a world, with nothing but the smell of books,
blind to the coming brewery of men
basking in the madness of their manliness.

Purple dance
(for Mr E)

I grew up with a boy in the backyard of Bochabela,
where boys played chibobo, and chickens ran free,
where women snorted snuff behind sun-soaked mud walls,
and houses spread like flattened cans.

He loved the hardness of a man's skin,
how it peered through the sheerness of a shirt,
his purple lipstick cracked creases across his lips,
and designed damage crusted like glue on his soul.

At times his cries were hiccups trapped by folds of fear;
potions and pills piled to the rafters of his red, red room,
as he cried like a bird beside an ebbing river.
His heart hurt like dough being sliced by baking soda.
He was as decent as silence on a hint of a feather,
handsome like a man masked with hands of hurt.

Coke and coffee on 5th floor

My brows furrow like a broom,
as I try to untangle your words
scattered like beads on the floor.
Your hands are wires poking the air,
your red toes shoot at the ceiling
as the purring fan starts to moan,

but you keep on talking.
My eyelids sweep my eyes,
damp sheets begging me to sleep.
You slurp another ocean of Coke,
a straw trembles on your lips.

I am fudge jammed to the couch,
my boobs sag as I slump
towards my cold coffee –
forgotten on a grainy floor,
as I listen to our friendship dying.

Slipping from me
(for Cassius, Eulander and Machaka)

I am mad that you've left me in hell,
that my curtains cover me with coldness
as I grow old without you.
I am angry with god and the sun and the cup
you were sipping from as you were slipping,
for they saw you slip with a chip of my heart
on the sleeve of your shirt and did not let me know.

Even Mziwabatho, the dog we raised
and chased in the wind, could not
sniff the whiff of your flight.
That day, inside our egg,
clouds were hanging like dough,
your red bell of silk splashed sexiness
to Tuku music stringing under a Baobab,
its shade lit by smiles of men with burdens
lost in the tunnels of their eyes,
as I coiled down to a ceiling of hell.

If I'd known that tea with me was your last,
I would have tied you to the ankles of my sink.
I feel betrayed by the tray that carried our teacups,
for not scratching the rupture of my laughter
as the tea went cold. I call your number, at times,
hoping this madness is just an ugly dress to take off.

Love on fire

I love Adhip, mama, his hair drips of Maghreb sands.
I'm happiness on fire. My madness is trapped on his tongue.
He does not break me like bread or fling me open like scissors.
His chest – a cocoon of hairs – not that stone that sawed my bones,
not slippery like Galela's gumboots.
My eyes claw on him as if sesame seeds on a bunny chow.
My love sweats the kind of madness you smell
in dogs on the run;

'My child, when you love in seconds like that,
your heart will be charcoal within an hour,
twisting in the oven to die like soot,
like boulder Galela who got weary of the yellow
you burnt on his chest. Fires like yours flare
up everywhere, in these shacks,
in Adhip's Atchar, in men so icy they slide
to the next house with rods writhing,
bleeding feelings like yours.
Your blasted heart
will hover over pages of this township
like the hunger we breathe to fill our guts.'

Lokshin pleasure

I like them rough around the cheeks,
smelling of tobacco, of soil.
They lurk around rusty corners.
They crawl out of shacks.
They taste of life,
and like it crispy, with a tinge of salt,
warm and round.
Yes: magwinya with snoek,
just the way pleasure should taste.

When women are train stations

The man had a woman at every station,
each perfumed in her township,
all oozing with the warmth of the bosoms
of their grandmothers.

Mahikeng had hugs; a sea of a dress
flaunting curves, hiding the hell
blazing in her chest as she swallowed
wrath with a pink-chalked smile.

Orkney wrapped hope in tight jeans,
after a few beers gulped
in a wind-shocked shack, too drunk to
sink into this hollow tube of a man,

a flower blooming behind a mine dump.
Her boobs, green apples;
her nipples, peanuts poking her T-shirt
to hooting taxis and GTIs,

grime of life under her white All Stars.
Orlando was older,
a pot of slow-cooking stew,
simmering, as future waited.

Tembisa was tea, trembling in a paper cup,
trying to live now,
teasing the Tom out of his train,
tearing its twigs apart.

Each station was more than his taste buds
could take,
leaving smoke to haunt the tracks of this train
of a man.

Bone of beauty

women like me, plain, wade through life,
become de door through which you walk;
gogo forgets my name, i'm de darkest ring of her eye,
i cut myself to feel felt. mama cuts my hair flat,
plaits/braids would waste her crumbs of time;

papa thinks i'm a silent mess.
friends flutter round him,
round de vastness of his laughter.
my calm hides behind mama's calm,
hers masked by dat bone of beauty.

if you fall
for me, you'll see I trail behind,
sniff past your heels for something deeper.
i crease to shine your shoes,
won't creep low to be crushed,
or reach high to dab your sweat.
you'll miss & hug me a bit,

den return to your bone of beauty,
she'll have de right name,
right job, play de game right
to swell her pocket & bloat your belly
as it pushes forward like a trolley in a mall;

i'm a skeleton hanging on your washing line
till it turns 100 & becomes a terrified stone of hell,
i eat no meat, chew no fear dat hides behind de fur of cows,
de knife shines past their eyeballs, lands on your plate,
music sears de fillet, not far from where Mbovana lies

in a sewer dat smells like posh foam bath,
her chest firecracker-tight,
time twisting above her,
next to a lipstick
too pink for her cocoa skin.

Ugly

He tells her no-one will be with a woman like her,
a baggage of long skirts scratching the gravel,
laced shoes padded for comfort, like a man's.
She says she feels like porcelain plunged into denim,
the world sees in her a wall littered with bricks.
She braids a mosaic with this shock, a wafer cracking
within a concert of rain, unpuddled, sloshing with lost
cloths and branches under the waters off Port Alfred,
where threads of jellyfish, squid and hair are stalking
a plastic cup that has a lipstick smirk smudged on it, still.
I tell you, nothing could be prettier than sewage
frothing and blinking with sea-life along the shoreline.
Underwater, her eyes start to crack like frozen marsh,
opening a tunnel scarier than the helplessness of living.

Your magic woman

The day you meet the woman you'll love,
and stumble upon her magic in the dark,
you'll remember how I used to drive
in the rain for hours to dry the palms
of your hands with my sweat,
how the black of your skin lit my eyes
– a mirror to your image –
an image carved by taxi rank crowds
framing you into a portrait of dignity.
The day you tumble into her mist,
my chest will be torn by stones
for all the hours I jazzed under
our passion-splashed umbrella.
The day you stumble into her fragrance,
my hands will have creased your brow.
All she'll see will be my love smudged on your face.
Time on wall calendars will leave you behind.

The shape of a man

I reach out to touch you, all I feel is wire.
Instead I kiss the breeze of your sighs.

How do you breathe surrounded by such hardness?
Or is this the shape of a man? A statue,
surrounded by moths under a lamppost?

The beat between your thighs,
the only warmth I ever felt from you.

I once had dis babé

'I'll see you soon babe',
he'd murmur down
my throat, straight to my pot,
but babé never did.

Maybe babé got broke,
high, hung over, hustled
hard or maybe the heavens
have him.

Seventy days later babé's
shadow's at my creaky door,
shocking its wail into silence.
'Babé I missed you!'

Dis babé, dis music of muscle
glistening in sliding sweat of desire,
wafting like real men
in Zamdela at dusk,

I once had dis babé,
dis packed mountain
of black diamond,
dirty, like coal,

hurling his forgotten self
in gum-boots, trying to dig
into my calabash of honey,
like that hole of hell
in shaft-two gold mine.

As you keep running

The wind rinses your name off my skin until I'm teaspoon clean
as distance morphs your train into sliding smoke.
Trekking by train to iBhayi cling-wraps time on your skin,
        time to live in your own ink
        and sink into what rubbers cannot erase.

Shosholoza-Meyl wobbles to a stop at stones called station-towns
dotted by huts, shepherds dragging gumboots and blue blankets
trailed by dogs with bare spines poking the sun. A trudging train
        can be a pain when fleeing from your own mess
        left tangled into steel-wool at our Sunday table.

I'll be forgetting about you, as you keep running.
By dusk I'll be perched on my tin roof like a wall on stilettos,
waiting for your bones to break at the edge of iBhayi
        as the lemon sun sinks into hues of orange,
        prunes, charcoal, as you explode alone.

Pain

When a lover moves on,
pain shines like plastic,
seeps into sandstone cracks,
and becomes wind.
When a friend departs
after her bone fails to heal,
the pain is wet-blanket heavy,
it clings to skin,
dries on a slate
the brave call healing.

Depression

Calm like a storm that's just ended,
it slides in like a cat's velvet feet,
covers her in warm liquid that forgets
to flee when the sun's skull crawls over
the spine of a waking mountain.
It sinks her into a pit, laces her eyes
white with soot, a soup of despair
frothing under her skin.
A spray of terror covers her, a sheet
that fled its bed in a nightmare.

The day she disappeared

He enters her kitchen like a wind from the Namib.
Pots clank in fear. Her face, a mature firm fruit,
becomes a fracture. There he stands, a rod on two legs.

Her fear is shreds of plastic trapped in barbed wire,
as his anger dances in the randomness of the room.
His slap slices her cheek like frozen rain,

she flies into the air, fear floods her floor; men
drinking beer outside have slid away like serpents,
her cries are strands of wool hiding in holes.

Later, she scrubs the smell of him off her dress,
gathers splattered pieces of herself from the ground,
flees behind the mountain where the sun hides.

Soldier in a black dress

Her marriage was a machine of sighs,
a cloud heaving in the air of her kitchen
before fists cracked it open
into a corner of obedience.

Before he died he became hollow,
started wearing a donkey's face.
Now he is crushed nothingness,
no loss dangling over his shadow.
Just flatness, a used tyre
drenched in the rain.

With nothing to mourn for,
the widow stands,
a soldier in black dress,
tasting the dryness of her tears.

Hanger

The cupboard wails like a dog
left alone in a garage.
My daughter's jersey lies there,
crying for its forgotten childhood.

A spider looks at me,
wires of web imprison her,
like a woman trapped
in the pages of her marriage.

I clasp the shirt of a man I once loved,
its frown slides between my fingertips,
weary from its life on a hanger,
time endless and terrifying.

One-way ticket

When he asks for me, tell him I'm under a silhouette of leaves,
to read a poem or two, in my mid-town accent.
I've dusted those raspberry boots that clasp the tightness of skin,
a calf more sinewy than lithe, if y'know what I mean.
Even the blue in my bedroom senses what's about to unravel.

Tell him I've gone to soften the hardness of words,
there by the rust and second-hand tyres.
I'm shreds; he'll have to be cloud to find me.
I'm in pozzies like Four-and-Six and Waaihoek.
My petticoat sheds off rags. They lie on a sidewalk, defeated –
That horizon across town is laced in my fragrance.

Tell him the stove's gone cold, the plates have stopped clanking,
my calf has slid into this stiletto suede the shade of blood.
Yep, the one I blew my fortnight wages on.
I'm taking a chance with the wind, for its flap seems to bat
like this one-way economy ticket in my hand.

My mother's house

When you lose your mother to death, you spend your life looking for her,
amongst small stones, on corners of your dishcloth, behind broken cars.
You fear throwing beans into a pot, lest she's there, hiding amongst them.

You carry your childhood everywhere: the comfort of overcooked food,
sugar on pumpkin pulp, oil in cabbage, doilies on the sofa.
You search for yourself all over: in books, in music, in corners of your nails.

I gaze at the sunset, hoping she will emerge, with her gait.
I feel her wide like an umbrella, try to clip her memory to my chest,
back to my childhood, back to the comfort of her food.

My knuckles crochet this din with the aid of mops and brooms.
Floors are shiny, bare, like peeled onion. Curtains bite their muteness
and the memory of people who are now plastic on walls.

Chairs are my four guests, a choir of owls sings carols on a TV screen.
An ant enters, looking for overcooked food,
next to knuckles of chairs, finding only fading religion.

Old houses

They carry the sadness
of burnt books,
graffiti of laughter left behind
in a haste of crammed boxes,
fragile walls held together
by rust-on-roof or sheer grace.

Old houses, wood floating
on a wafer of steel and change,
always eager to absorb
the next tenant's warmth.

Old timer

My wife's memory
>wakes me from the hard-boiled egg of my bed.
>My heart's still stuck to the boniness of my knee.
>I turn the bathroom tap on, it coughs, a memory
>>slides out.

My face
>looks like pain, a path that swallows itself
>into a burnt-out candle, goes to bed with darkness,
>with hope, wakes up alone. Even death
>>has fled me.

My sons' sons
>burst through the paper of my walls
>like a seven-pronged knife.
>their music: an enamel dish on my red stoep
>>scraping soil.

The War Up North (1944/5)

Soldiers Without Reward (J.S. Mohlamme)

Malome was gone before his voice hissed like a kettle,
before he bore children who bounced
with candles on evening walls.
His last gasp slid into wood, like a sword in some desert.

Sergeants' boots arrived at his mother's door,
with dry faces, a bicycle, two pounds and a coat,
like memory on a stretcher.
The coat's label seemed to say: 'warm wash,
do not iron, ride & wear like an idea of slashed wood.'

She hissed, like a kettle, for a soldier without an award.

A bus for the dying

I make a living stretching old people's minds,
  one of whom has his last hours flowing
    over the edge, December ramming into January
      with no champagne glasses to break the shroud of old year
His eyes pierce a window as if scratching a stone.

'Finally, it's here!' he darts about like a butter knife.
  Pins of delight pierce the crease of his skin
    as the bus empties stoeps and yards along its trail
      Missus' scalp is plucked like a hen's after snipping
her locks for a girl whose marrow was shrunk by an illness.

As the bus coughs to a halt, Missus' dress wears its shimmer,
  a flower etches redness into the satin skin of her bag,
    the old man's cheeks apricoting a roundness
      that carries his lightness out of the House for the Aged
        We musketeer in, as puppy paws bid us
goodbye on the hoarseness of a dorpie road.

The bus is filled with lives beyond a brim of knowing,
  their costumes and suits keeping this sand from spilling over,
    One ol' timer's tobacco pipe puffs and horns out like an impala's
      A woman in a flurry of perfume nimbles in
with an impatience of a rain-sniffing wind.

Along the city terrace a young man's concertina stretches
  his locust ribs, his eyes orange from cocaine ash
    Tyres swerve shot-left, skipping him this time
      His mom salt-rains to the floor, knees shattering in relief
as she hears her husband's foil-wrapped skin un-crease.

The bus groans up a koppie's gravel road,
  a widow drooping with library books
    and cat food debt hails it,
      but she - too - broke - to - die
so we leave her there, hardening like a rock.

Clothes peddler

I stop by to sell wares that fell from a wagon
at Dunuza, just below Park Station's ankles,
or acquired for ten bucks in a house buried
under oak shades. My wares carry a whiff
of the salt of the sea that disembarked
with them. The men's eyes scratch the hems,
looking for double stitching, a sign the pants
can stand the grind of life.

The men's handsomeness
is etched into a wall of stone,
shorts creaseless, shoes wood-polished,
sneakers so cotton-clean you wonder
how the brown of the earth escaped them.
They're looking for odd jobs, without
cardboards scrawled *Painting*, or *Welding*,
they are drenched in faith, something
more baffling to me than hope.

They sense that one pair once had a jacket,
is a missing part of something,
a reason to lower the price, I guess.
There's no glory in a skewer of slacks
swollen by so many legs. I remain a haggler
pushing a wagon of wares.

Mamboshwa looking for work

She stands at my door, her raincoat drenched in despair,
her shoes pumpkin-pulp wet, sunken in another existence,
her energy on my green peppers and tomatoes.
The mess of cents, of sweat, after selling sweets.
Plans pour out of her bra: snuff, fahfee numbers, ten rand note, hope.
She unpegs words, as if from a washing line, her teeth mealie pieces

bitten off by a toothless man. Behind me my paw-paw seeds huddle
in their wetness, scared, like her. Her sacks, boxes of exhaustion,
fence her in, shield her from my man's stare, landing
like a flash on her ankles, as his whiff of espresso, of after-shave,
guards our middle-class comfort. Maybe later she'll arrive home
to a room full of people. And no-one will stare.

Slay queen broken on heels

There's something about her that's like mud.
You mould her into what she could become,
she remains a stone sitting between winds.

At times she's a mess on crack-coke,
a dot sinking into a damp cloth,
a wind to be built again in the morning.

There's something baffling about that,
about a woman walking on pricks,
hearing her bones break to pieces,

thudding thicker than a knuckle,
the sound of a bubble fleeing a boulder
for something that's eaten her tongue.

Mashonisa at dawn

The morning's cotton wool hovers around his fence.
His face resembles lines of the bark
of a tree he leans against.
Television jabbers, fills a void it can't understand.
A crack of vetkoek, a hum of tea.

Men in coats, gold teeth & Florsheim shoes
emerge from a gusheshe,
like coins from holes and pockets.
In the distance, dogs wail like presences in sealed flour tins.
A wall of coats and gold teeth surrounds him,
as he sweats like plastic clinging around his shack.

Basket's day at work

Route 59's cars slide by, their occupants buffered
in comfort. Only Piet's truck staggers to a halt,
wary of radio-man spilling words into his ears.
On this hiking hoek, you become scissors tucked
in boots (and not that umbrella skirt that flares up)
for that climb up the truck seat needs legs of steel,
or winds will blow you away like a nest into
mielie fields, and back to where you started.

Ou Piet is travelling Up North to Beit Bridge,
his truck tumbles you out near railway tracks.
You snip off lavender heads on a road
littered with lives too real to be etched
in books or movies or statues of bronze,
lives that carry grease under fingernails.

Your soil-gripped boots pant, and pause,
under a sackcloth full of overalls of men.
Zam-Bucked, lips saucer-flat on mageu's brim,
you gulp what remains of the trek.
Across the rails, houses squeeze on mielie cobs,
H-A-A-K   V-R-Y-S-T-A-A-T chokes old windmill.
'Why d'you keep going to a woman's
warmth?' Ghost asks Basket, 'when you can heal
within tobacco winds, next to a muscle of men?'

Night chores await you in washrooms,
you wax soap on khaki, to rid it of smells
that remind you you're alive and rotting.
Ou Marie enters, honeyed, cinnamoned,
tousling fragrant things, thrusting sticks,
next to skin, between braces of your bra:
a hint of koeksuster, of naartjie.

'I'm Ou Marie, a Route 59 ghost,
all day 'been tryin to tell you:
you're a basket, jong,
you carry things you'll never have.
And your home?
Wherever there's a roof.'

Looking for Bra Satch on payday

We leave in our vastness, eyes yellow in haste
towards Number 1 Hostel, a typical day of tea,
babies-on-breasts, warmth-on-winter-walls.
Sometimes pastors bawl inside sweating tents.
But not today.

Men with cash pour from houses,
to hang with majita at the Hostel
– that tomb of beds with blankets rolled like hay,
hiding a spoon and some chipped cup and plate –
'Bra Satch was here just now,' they say.
He's everywhere-and-nowhere,
between corridors cracking from music.

Around a bend, air spits mbaola sparks,
as arms of a muscle-of-a-man flex.
'Bopha, Mzalwane!' ma-grootman cheer on,
their cheeks parched like plastic drying in its own time,
men who've had to forget the contours of a woman.
Men nothing like Bra Satch, with pockets chequered with cash.

Payday at Skoti Phola

That night, music blared to pot bellies,
we were dancing to nothing, bobbing like two boats.

My man's mint tobacco trapped in folds
of a leather jacket, Lion matchstick stuck to his mouth.

Life splashed on his face.
The hardness of wood, of his veins,
of things he refused to become.

Two beer quarts guarded the dance
of paraffin on a primus stove, as the sun slid down.

Outside, a bus sneezed coats of men, makarapa, gumboots.

Don't die like I did
(last words to my sister)

Do not love your man, or your scent
will bend inside his skull like heat
trapped in folds of cabbage.
He will smell you in the coffee
that comforts his loud mouth.
He will slice you each time he
bats the butter on his bread.
Do not let him love you for long,
or you'll be a lump in his throat
each time he coughs.

Freedom is the right to sleep under
leaking roofs where soil melts
after it has rained and rained.
Your heart is a red panty on that
washing line, behind that boiling
shack that packs us like tinned fish.

Here in Freedom Park hearts crush in the air,
even flowers are not innocent, babies' heads
crack walls like lost balls of chibobo,
mothers' eyes are holes poked into an abyss,
deaf to the silence of death dragging at their beds,
as men pelt their bones black with belts
and leave them to walk like bats.

Last year, I died, and saw my late father,
a man who, when I was four, sang me songs,
with a dompas glued to his pocket,
hiding his hopping heart.
Mashamplan had just burnt my beauty with a bang.
Bang! Bang! a stutter of hard beans fled his gun,
turning my face into a messed-up piece of meat.
I then died and rhymed again with our dead father.

Today the beast is dead. Bang! Bang! in the head.
Mashamplan. is. dead.
To his dying ear I say: 'Your scent has been an event in my grave,
waiting for you to blast it off my bald bones, in this skunk box
that's been my home since that Bang! in my head.'

The looting

Shah's heart hides behind the peel of his skin
close to his fears as layers of men, hands,
women, nails, breathe each other's haste in his shop,
ripping out its bowels like yolk from a mother's shell.

Crushed cash counters lie below crates of Cola
staggering out of this pencil-scribbled chaos
spilling into gaping mouths of houses, hunger
and babàlaas, leaving windows stunned
as stories swarm like ants.

We're forty years old looking like marbles
lost inside Shah's shop, baffled by anger
tearing us into threads of chicken flesh,
waking up to live for nothing except to chase
grains of hate toasting in the stupor of space.

Manana is cold

Her body is a little knot under a damp cloth
on Dolo Road, a lamp of silence covers her. Or is it God?
A throat of hushed voices, in thirsty bushes, amongst dead gates,
as fear cracks her chest into prayers of a Friday of Songs,
next to a mini-loaf taxi that darted at her like a blind hippo.

Dread drums Manana's papa's ears, pain trapped in his eyes like peas.
Our lips slice open to say nothing to him, as he fades into a cinder.
We tuck our blankets into corners of our round waists,
baffled like potatoes abandoned in the air.

She lies there, bare like a baby bird, on a road too cold for her.
We swallow words, for winds lashed a father's heart at 1pm.
Manana is gone. We fold our words like envelopes, stand like chairs.

Geelbooi's homecoming

He enters, a 1970's relic, through an imagination of a gate,
a memory of an Afro, of Percy Sledge
sliding in circles between songs of an LP record player.
Ten yellow hairs fray on his balding lawn's scalp,
below rusting roofs, next to upturned paint tins
on which ageing men sit over drinks,
behind cigarette smoke, like wheelbarrows,
like things useful only at funerals.

Embers wink, sink into ash.
Furrows between their brows unfold like tablecloths,
to recall a name, a childhood, a memory,
while women with strong feet and big chests carry
the meat of a freshly-cut-up sheep that had been
breathing and peeing on a red stoep an hour ago.
Aunts, unwed aunts' daughters, pour out,
chests bouncing ahead of them, towards this feather.
Uncles trail behind on borrowed feet of ants,
to greet Geelbooi, a hut that's slowing crumbling.

Biza, Ou Kop & Tiger stagger next to Black Label quarts.
'Jerr, G, ke wena motho o?'
'Jaanong ha o tsohetse jaana, monna?'
Their chuckles smear a stainless-steel tray with
missing teeth.
'Was it 1989 when you left?'
Suddenly my heart starts to hurt as if
there's a needle threading through it.

IV

First words

It was a place where dung was paint
and polish and smelled like pot.
I slid towards my peeling door,
towards sunshine bursting
with second chances.

I smelled the dawn and the dust,
the gutters and the dying dogs,
the donkeys and the brewing beer,
skomfana, mfana.
Then, with heaven in my hands,
I began to write.

The reading

The audience is lit light-bulbs,
their paw-paw thoughts
inside lit lanterns.
One of the thoughts scrapes
a mole sitting on my nose
before leaping to grip a rafter
where spiders are mending
frayed Sparapara letters.
My teeth spit pieces of paper.
Startled by the tank of me,
lanterns start to float out
till they're silver slits
sitting on a liquorice sky
– I'm berry slush –
A mop wipes my mess off
stage, and just like that,
I disappear.

Yellow shade

My door opens to the outside like the mouth
of a woman waiting for a man
who never arrives from the dust of a diamond pit.

Lemons dangle from my tree like young breasts.
The tree yields to birds, the sun hangs on top of branches,
its yellow creeping through hissing leaves.

Tired women in overalls perch under this yellow shade.
Some have hair the hardness of little stones,
others' locks fray in the wind, fleeing their eyes.
Stones are there for company too.

Fish slice through water, as shrubs shiver.
Talk overflows, whispering the spirits of //Hu!Gaeb
inside the chests of women whose skin is the shade of clay.
Like soil, scent of their names is everywhere.

I had plans

I had plans for the day death came.
I was going to swim in the river
like paper; swirl like soft porridge
on my granny's table.

I was going to watch the sun crack
through the peeling door,
like a mirror running away
from a car hauled by a ghost.

I was going to grace the sandstone skull
of Thaba Bosiu; smell the dignity
of my father's cattle,
their hides shimmering in the sun.

But then I passed away.

Death slid like a curtain.
Mourners howled hymns inside
my hut, the way women do
when they need their husbands

to shut up. I told them they had banged
on the wrong door. So they folded arms
into a tight stack of wood; and allowed
darkness to blanket my being.

And then I passed away.

I want to live

I want to live where socks soak in the colour of copper,
where doors creak like skin ungluing from a night's sleep,
as I look through a window dripping with rain that unties a knot
jabbing my heart.

I crave cocoa with cream and scones folded in butter,
the road so far away that cars are a haze of ants trailing,
harmless. I crave potatoes freckled with brown mud
crumbling off their skin,

warm and damp between my fingers, dug up from earth beneath
my window sill. I long for heaven, lest there's none above my head,
in case it's hiding inside the memory of Malaisha the Trafficker,
as his kombi's legs

break down under stacked luggage, behind Beit Bridge thorns,
far from the sea of a city housing people inside long rods of teeth
grinning in the blue vacuum of the sky, its myth inside the glass
yard of their minds.

I hark back to the dampness of wood, feet dirty-warm
in a puddle that knows it'll soon be mud, my heart unzipping
to rain spitting, as I sharpen a pencil to hear
what charcoal tales it will tell.

NOTES

p.11 *Middle-town*
ntate – a term of respect used to refer to a man
moruti – a preacher

p.12 *Far from home*
thôbane – a wooden walking stick with a round knob on top

p.14 *The lure of liquid delight*
skomfana – local word for a home-brewed alcoholic African beer
made mainly from sorghum; see also p.59

p.16 *Purple dance*
Bochabela – one of the oldest townships in Mangaung
chibobo or shibobo – a popular soccer tactic where a player tricks an
opponent by passing a ball between his/her legs; see also p.52

p.21 *Slipping from me*
Tuku music – the music of Zimbabwean musician Oliver Mtukudzi,
who died in Harare in 2019 at the age of 66. He sang in Shona,
Ndebele and English, and recorded more than 60 albums.

p.23 *Lokshin pleasure*
lokshin – common term for any historically black South African
township (also known as a location or kasie)

p.24 *When women are train stations*
GTIs – Volkswagen Golf cars popular with young urban men

p.30 *As you keep running*
Shosholoza Meyl – long distance passenger train

p.36 *One-way ticket*
pozzie(s) – a local hangout/house or home
Four-and-Six – part of Batho, the oldest existing black township in
Mangaung. It derives its name from the 1919 wage dispute campaign
in which workers demanded a daily living wage of 4s/6d (four
shillings and six pence)

Waaihoek – one of the earliest townships in Bloemfontein, established in the mid-1800's and demolished in the 1920's after forced removals. It is also the place where the African National Congress was founded in 1912

p.42 *The War Up North (1944/5)*
This poem is based on a story about my maternal great-uncle, who perished in the war that South Africa took part in as part of allied countries fighting Nazi Germany in WWII. We were told that his brother, my grandfather, who did survive the war, was given a bicycle and a coat. In the poem I also allude to 'two pounds' that J.S. Mohlamme indicates the returnee black soldiers were given as a once-off allowance. For further reading on South African soldiers' participation in WWII, see:
Mohlamme, J.S. (1995). Soldiers without Reward: Africans in South Africa's Wars. *Military History Journal,* vol. 10, no. 1, June 1995.
Moloi, V. (2007). *A Pair of Boots and a Bicycle.* A documentary film on Job Maseko, a highly decorated South African soldier who fought in WWII.

p.43 *A bus for the dying*
musketeer – my term for moving in threes, as in the 'The Three Musketeers', the 19th century novel by Alexandre Dumas

p.46 *Slay queen broken on heels*
slay queen – a young glamorous woman with expensive tastes

p.47 *Mashonisa at dawn*
mashonisa – money lenders or cash loans
gusheshe – an old model of a 325i BMW car that enjoys an iconic status in South African townships

p.48 *Basket's day at work*
hoek – corner (Afrikaans)
mageu – a non-alcoholic sour drink popular in southern Africa. It is made from fermented maize porridge
Haak Vrystaat – rugby term generally used by Free Staters to encourage or motivate a team or any group of people

p.50 *Looking for Bra Satch on payday*
mbaola – a brazier
bopha – to fasten or bind
mzalwane – a fellow Christian or born-again Christian
magrootman – (typically used by younger men to refer to) older men

p.51 *Payday at Skoti Phola*
Skoti Phola – part of a residential settlement in Mangaung
makarapa – plastic protective helmet for mineworkers; also popular
with soccer fans

p.52 *Don't die like I did*
dompas – 'dumb pass' or 'stupid pass' (Afrikaans) ; the pass book or
reference book that all black people over the age of 16 were forced to
carry in apartheid times, in order to regulate their daily lives

p.54 *The looting*
babalaas – a hangover

p.56 *Geelbooi's homecoming*
Jerr, ke wena motho o? – my goodness, is it really you?
Jaanong ha o tsohetse jaana monna? – man, now why do you look so
old?

p.59 *First words*
mfana – a boy (isiZulu)

p.60 *The reading*
sparapara – slang for staffriding, a form of train surfing where young
men would climb on, disembark from and climb back on a moving
train for the thrill of it, thus making a parapara sound as their feet tap
on the platform. In 'The reading', Sparapara refers to Staffrider, a South
African writers' magazine (1978-1993), which had a spin-off series that
published novels, short stories, poetry, as well as photography

p.61 *Yellow shade*
//Hu!Gaeb – pre-colonial Khoe-Sān name for Cape Town

Printed in the United States
by Baker & Taylor Publisher Services